This Spending Log Belongs to:

www.ingramcontent.com/pod-product-compliance
Lightning Source LLC
Chambersburg PA
CBHW021356210526
45463CB00001B/115
* 9 7 8 1 7 9 3 0 7 7 9 1 2 *